Montu Dhillon is a licensed real estate sales representative in Ontario, Canada. Montu Dhillon is not a licensed attorney, lawyer, tax advisor, or any other licensed professional. Anyone considering implementing these ideas and plans are advised to seek professional advice concerning legal and tax matters.

Copyright © 2020 Montu Dhillon

No part of this book may be reproduced, stored in a retrieval system, or transmitted by any means without the written permission of the author.

TABLE OF CONTENTS

1   INTRODUCTION

5   WHAT YOU MUST KNOW WHEN BUYING PRE-CONSTRUCTION CONDOS

19   HOW REAL ESTATE PROFESSIONALS MAKE PRE-CONSTRUCTION CONDOS INTO SOLID INVESTMENT PROPERTIES

33   TOP TIPS TO SELL A PROPERTY FAST AND FOR THE VALUE YOU WANT

53   SECRETS OF FINANCING ON YOUR TERMS

INTRODUCTION

PRE-CONSTRUCTION CONDOMINIUMS ARE A HOT INVESTMENT.

By hot, I don't mean pre-construction condos are popular.

You won't see them as the subject of cable TV shows. Most real estate agents won't even talk about them – that is unless you bring the subject up with them. (It exposes that they aren't industry insiders.)

No, what makes preconstruction condos hot is that they're an exceptionally simple way to get a new property at a low cost to own, rent, or sell for a BIG profit.

Savvy real estate insiders scoop them up as fast as they become available. This is especially true in growing cities like Toronto where developers are putting up new condos in highly desirable areas, making them ideal properties for a primary residence, vacation home, or – my personal favorite – as a rental property.

In this book, you will find the secrets insider's use to acquire, sell, invest and profit from preconstruction condos.

Inside, you'll also find a lot of bonus content, so you can be as savvy as those making a ton of money investing in real estate, be it preconstruction condos or any other type of real estate opportunity.

Whether you're looking for a home, second home or investment property, I'm going to share how you can make the biggest possible profit in a real estate investment.

You don't need to make the mistakes I made!

INTRODUCTION

I started off buying and then renting single-family homes. That was ok. Soon after, I started rehabbing distressed properties and flipping them for "profit." If you've done this, you know exactly what I mean by "profit" - a lot of headaches, loads of work, and only meager rewards.

In the end, and for all my money invested…for all my blood and sweat…for all my troubles chasing contractors to complete a job …all I would yield after six months was a measly $18,000.

After taxes, I realized I would have made more money working at Starbucks for 6 months!

Meanwhile, during the entire process, I saw real estate agents doing a little work and making more per transaction than us entrepreneurs. And at the end of the job, I would sometimes discover my property had a leaky roof or foundation.

Renovation projects always seemed to be a dollar short and a day late. *For example…*

On one project, I personally kept an eye on the team working on the renovation. I visited the condo unit every 3 days, only to find no progress. This went on for weeks!

It turned out the crew was not showing up on their dedicated days, or they called in sick, or whatever - for 3 solid weeks. Here I was paying the carrying costs and no work was being done.

Now, the young me would have had a shouting match with the General Contractor. The older-and-wiser me simply said, "I'm going to hold back 10% of the contract until the job is done. And for every day you go past the promised finish date, I'm going to deduct $150 for my carrying costs."

Yes, you can bet that they finished that job in a hurry then!

*But…*for all the pain, toil, and trouble, that $18,000 reward hardly seemed worth it.

At the time, I was also buying bungalows outside of the city and renting them out. The caveat here was these lower rent accommodations were attracting a lower caliber tenants and bigger headaches.

My greatest lesson was when I took ownership of a house in Cambridge, Ontario, assuming the existing Tenancy. The tenant on the lease skipped out. His jobless friend moved in instead. Now altruistic me decided to give him a chance. After all, he already had his stuff moved in, what could go wrong?

Here's what happened…

He didn't pay rent for 2 months. He had no money as he had no work (he had moved in with no job). I remember looking him dead in the eyes and saying, "I know you feel life has been unfair to you, so I'm going to give you one chance to turn it around and fix it. It starts by meeting your obligations for this unit. Don't mistake my kindness for weakness, if you don't come through, I won't go easy on you. What's it going to be?"

He nervously agreed and scratched his shirtless belly in the heat of that July afternoon. For all his twitchy nods, he didn't come through.

When I started the eviction process via Sheriff and all the other appropriate authorities, he knew the system and was able to delay the eviction by 40 days. He claimed to the Landlord Tenant Board that I had interrupted his reasonable enjoyment of the home.

(Did I mention, he used a fake name and never provided me with ID.)

Anyway, he stole a trailer and left it in the driveway. He trashed the kitchen. Later I learned he was arrested for carrying a concealed weapon in his car, which he claimed was a BB gun. Oh, and he had drug-related charges on his record…

INTRODUCTION

When he was finally evicted, it cost me $1,000 JUST for the garbage removal he left behind. And the ONLY reason I succeeded in getting him out was that he got arrested and had to spend a month in jail!

All in all, this lesson cost me $8,000 and took 5 months. But that's cheap compared to some other stories I've heard about nightmare tenants.

Then one day, by serendipity or providence, everything changed.

An acquaintance, let's call her Lisa, told me that the best decision she ever made was buying a pre-construction condo, a condo unit sold by a builder before the beginning of construction. Developers sell these units in advance to raise funds for the project, what's called a pre-construction sale.

Now, sometimes you'll see units being sold throughout construction. As you'll see in a moment, you want to buy before that, as an insider, and you want to buy as early as possible in a pre-construction project.

Why?

Well, Lisa told me she made $150,000 profit on the sale of her preconstruction condo. And she did nothing more than sign a few papers and buy the thing.

I couldn't believe it.

To prove her wrong, and secretly hoping she was right, I decided to give it a try, just in case it was as easy as she claimed.

Over the four years of construction, I signed a few checks and made the deposit requirements. Then, when it was ready, I closed and sold it for $200,000 in profit.

Not a bad gain for only signing a few checks! And

it certainly beats fixing up old houses from dawn to dusk.

Since then I've redirected my investment strategy to finding the best pre-construction condo projects that offer the biggest returns. And I am repeating the same success, over and over.

And now…
I want to help you do the same!

My start with real estate investment was full of frustration. One of the biggest struggles I faced was getting the right information. I wanted to know if the property was a good buy. Instead, all I got was a high-pressure sales pitch.

Let me tell you, nothing pushes me out the door faster…

And I don't want you to go through this.

After more than a decade of investing in real

INTRODUCTION

estate, I want to help you reap the immense financial and personal rewards of investing in real estate, particularly with pre-construction condo buying.

I've tried many things, and the reason I focus on this niche is that it's the easiest vehicle with the least hassle. Nothing, absolutely nothing is like pre construction condo investing. Do you know what all the wealthy people in the world have in common? Especially the 1%? They all own real estate.

· If you're buying a home, you'll find out how to lock in amazingly low prices so you're almost guaranteed exceptional appreciation by the time you're moving in.

· If you're buying to sell, you'll know where to buy, how to buy and when to buy for the biggest profit.

· If you're getting an investment property, you'll learn how to minimize your investment and maximize its value as a rental.

In short, with this book you have access to the same information real estate insiders like me have spent years – and money – learning. And if you need one on one help, you can contact me or someone from my team. As experienced real estate mentors, we have guided many people just like you to financial freedom. Just contact us via www.dhillonrealtysystems.ca, or give me a call at 1-833-845-5674.

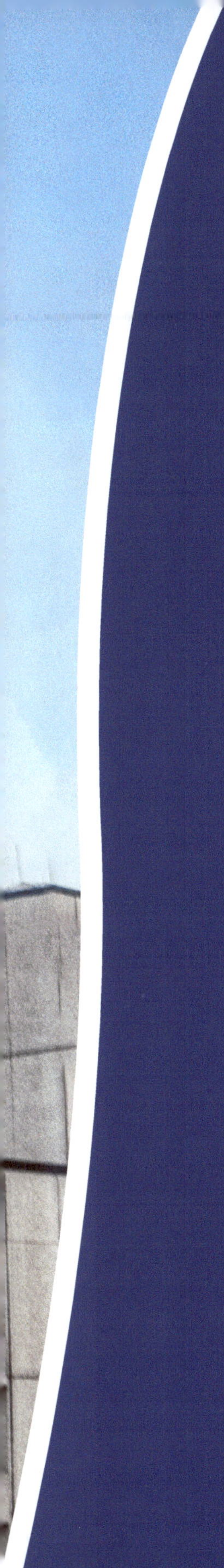

WHAT YOU MUST KNOW WHEN BUYING PRE-CONSTRUCTION CONDOS

WHY INSIDER'S LOVE THEM,
WHAT TO EXPECT WHEN BUYING,
AND HOW TO GET THE BEST VALUE

WHY REAL ESTATE INSIDERS LOVE TO BUY PRE-CONSTRUCTION CONDOS

In the introduction, I highlighted that huge profit potential was a big reason why me and my friends love pre-construction condos. Admittedly, it's probably the biggest reason I buy.

But it isn't the only reason.

Here are 7 more benefits I've identified that make pre-construction condos a superior investment:

1) Affordability. Condos are one of the most affordable housing options around. A pre-construction VIP sale can get a unit for 5%-10% off its initial public price.

2) A safer investment. A new condo is a tangible, physical asset that always has value. Sure, prices can fluctuate depending on demand, but as a long-term investment, it is much safer than stocks and bonds. Plus, you can turn it into a revenue producer as a rental.

3) It's new! You, or whoever you rent to, gets to enjoy all the benefits that come with living in a totally new and up-to-date building, with cutting edge modern technology built into it.

4) Makes for an exceptional rental property. It's new and needs little if any maintenance or updating once it's ready. In other words, it's the easiest way to get started with rental properties. In Toronto and the Greater Toronto Area, rental values continue to rise.

5) Customizing is easy. Do you want your unit to have a unique "something?" By buying during the pre-construction phase, you can add special upgrades and finishes to make it "home sweet home" or a highly desirable rental property.

6) Fewer headaches than buying a fixer-upper. Really, I should say no headaches. Here's what I mean…with the fixer-upper, you do all the work, or at least struggle coordinating it. With new construction, you sit back and let the pros do it. At most you might need to pick which finish or any special add-ons you want.

7) Signing is easy and risk-free. Yes, risk-free. In fact, nothing is easier than the signing process to buy a pre-construction condo. Let's take a closer look at that process…

YOUR PRE-CONSTRUCTION BUYING PROCESS

In Toronto, the pre-construction sales process typically follows these five different phases.

1. **Friends and Family go first**. These are the developers family members and previous clients. They typically get the first option on units, but guess what, builders don't typically release the best units at this time!

The best and most desirable units are sold later - at a premium!

Most buyers go in at this stage **without** an experienced agent to represent them. It's not necessarily that they don't want an agent, rather, agent representation is not permitted during the Friends and Family phase.

That might sound odd, but it's the way it is. And frankly, it's in the builder's best interest. I can't tell you how many times I've heard of friends and family not being familiar with the fine print and later receiving unpleasant surprises in the form of unexpected costs as they get close to closing.

2. **Platinum brokers go next**. Developers give platinum brokers, the special privilege of selling a set block of units. With a Platinum broker, you get the same pricing as Friends and Family and access to floor plans before anyone else. Platinum brokers typically receive a set allocation of reserved units and whatever they do not sell goes back into the builder's inventory for the next phase.

3. **VIP brokers come next**. These brokers sell for the developer but not quite as much as platinum brokers. Prices tick upwards slightly, and some premium units are released here. Higher floors, corner units, premium views, etc.

4. **Regular realtors have the next option to go in with their clients.** You can go in with your family's realtor, but this does not guarantee the highest priority access to units. In fact, you're only one step above the general public and you certainly pay a higher price than Platinum/VIP brokers, and family and friends.

5. **Everyone else, aka the General Public**. Finally, when the last 15% of units remain, the general public has their chance to buy.

For the best pricing and value, you want to buy your preconstruction condo through a Platinum or VIP broker, if you aren't one yourself. This access gets you the best price with priority selection of available units, so you can get that corner unit with an awesome view or one closer to the elevator, say if you're renting it out.

To get this VIP treatment, you need to find a real estate broker or agent with these inside connections. That's how real estate insiders who don't want to go through the hassle of becoming licensed do it themselves.

SIGNING FOR YOUR PRECONSTRUCTION CONDO

Signing is *really* simple. Better yet, you only need a very small investment to get started.

· First, your broker completes a worksheet to reserve your unit. All you need to do is provide your broker/agent with a copy of your ID.

Here's the thing…a worksheet is not a binding contract. If you decide after completing the worksheet that you don't want it. Fine, you don't have to make the purchase.

· Next, you meet with the developer and sign the contract, the Agreement of Purchase and Sale. At this step, you also make a small deposit, usually around $5,000.

But you still have no risk!

"Wait a minute. How can that be?" you might be asking.

It has everything to do with a "cooling-off period."

You can walk into a developer's office, sign the contract without reading it and give them the check without fear. You have a 10 day (calendar days, not business days) period to review the agreement and reconsider your purchase.

If you decide in those 10 days this really isn't for you, there are no penalties. *All you need to do is call and say you want to cancel the agreement. You'll get your check returned and then get on with your life.*

Sound too good to be true?

Maybe. But those are the rules and sometimes (just sometimes) the rules work in your favor.

Now, during this "cooling-off period," I always recommend my clients have their attorneys review the contract. This avoids any unwanted surprises. I've never seen any contract problems, but a legal review can identify any potential concerns unique to your situation or investment goals.

· The final step involves no work. If the contract's good, you do nothing. After 10 days, the contract goes into effect.

That's it.

You might remember, I mentioned that when I bought and sold my first preconstruction condo, all I did was sign a few checks. Well, once the agreement is in place, here's typically how it goes.

- Around 30 days after signing, you make a 5% payment.
- 120 days later you pay another 5%.
- At 9 months (270 days), you'll write a check for your next 5%.

- When construction is completed several years later and the unit is ready for occupancy, you make the final 5% payment. But you still don't own the condo at this point.

The entire building must be completed and registered as a condo corporation before they transfer the title to you. That's when you get a mortgage and pay the closing costs.

So, your first three payments typically stretch across nine months. The final payment could be months or even years later.

All I did was sign a few checks.

It really is just this easy.

WHAT HAPPENS IF SUDDENLY I CAN'T AFFORD IT?

I hope this never happens to you but should it, you do have options. Developers often include a way for a buyer to assign, or sell their unit, to someone else. A real estate broker and a good attorney can make sure your contract includes this clause.

HOW SOON CAN I MOVE IN, AKA WHAT IS INTERIM OCCUPANCY?

You get to live in or rent out your unit before you take the title, this is when construction of your suite is complete but others on higher floors are not. This often includes an interim occupancy fee. Interim occupancies can be for a couple of months or even go up to a couple of years. It all depends on which floor you are on.

WHAT REAL ESTATE INSIDERS LOOK FOR WHEN BUYING

"Montu," my client leaned in close, just a few inches away from my ear.

Then she whispered, "I want something cheap, facing the water, it has to be big, near all the amenities, in the downtown core. Can you make it happen?"

"My dear," I replied with a gentle gaze towards the horizon, "If that existed, I would buy it and you would never hear of it."

…

In real estate, you can have 2 out of these 3:
Fast. Cheap. Well Built. But NEVER all three.

Preconstruction condos are no exception, especially in the Greater Toronto Area. Even so, it's still a big investment deserving of careful consideration.

For example, as North America's 4th largest city – and it's still growing – Toronto represents one of the most diverse and dynamic areas in the world. It contains…

HIGH DEMAND FOR HOUSING IN TORONTO.

· The presence of world-class universities meaning a student population, ie., potential renters.

· Abundant cultural opportunities that attract tourists.

· A dynamic downtown and lively nightlife, adding value to nearby properties.

· A destination city for Canadians and those moving to Canada from all around the globe.

As a growing city, you have a lot of options including where in the city you might choose to make your preconstruction purchase?

THINGS TO CONSIDER WHEN BUYING:

- <u>Why You're Buying</u>. Are you buying for yourself, to sell, or will it be a rental property? Whatever your reason, you want to make sure you research the markets and locations that promise the best return (or access) for you.

Access is big. You might like the idea of owning a high-rent property near the city center, but if you live outside the city, are you going to be okay traveling in every time you need to meet new renters?

- <u>How soon you want the unit</u>. Are you looking for an immediate place to live or revenue producer? Your timeframe for taking ownership plays a big part in where to look.

- <u>How much you want to invest</u>. You might be able to get a condo in a highly sought-after area of the city for much lower than the market price, but that doesn't mean it doesn't come with a big price tag! Affordability is always a big part of any investment. The best choice is always the one that meets your current financial situation.

- <u>Lifestyle choices</u>. If buying for yourself, you want a place that matches your desired lifestyle – the nightlife of downtown, a family setting, or maybe a place to retire. If you're looking to rent, who are your ideal renters? Students? If so, buy close to a university. Tourists/ travelers? Buy near downtown or near public transportation.

There are many factors to consider. Talk to a successful real estate investor and you'll find they have a team behind them. At a minimum, they work with an attorney and a well-connected agent.

WHAT YOU MUST KNOW WHEN BUYING PRE-CONSTURCTION CONDOS

AS YOU LOOK TO MAXIMIZE YOUR INVESTMENT, HERE ARE THE 10 STEPS I RECOMMEND EVERYONE DO BEFORE SIGNING FOR A PRECONSTRUCTION CONDO.

1. MAKE SURE YOU'RE WORKING WITH A BUYER'S AGENT.

Here's a good point to remember:

A platinum broker has earned this position by knowing a lot about the available product and selling a lot for the developer.

If an agent represents the developer, he or she is a seller's agent. If the agent works for you at no cost, then you're working with a buyer's agent. If you can find a buyer's agent who has connections with developers, you're going to be in good shape.

Plus, a buyer's agent can become a good partner and represent you best by knowing your needs and being knowledgeable about neighborhoods, construction, warranties, financing, differences in pricing, quality, even unit selection, so that you get the best value for your money.

2. GET IN TOUCH WITH YOUR AGENT.

Before you set out to explore the area where the condo is going up, sit down with your agent and do your homework. Getting a little inside information can save you time by determining whether the new condos fit within a comfortable price range.

How to Know Your Comfortable Price Range

Comfortable property prices for homes and preconstruction condos are two entirely different things. Due to their low upfront costs, you can get a high-value property with little down, but…eventually you will need to afford the balance.

Talk it over with your real estate agent.

- If you're planning on buying and eventually moving in, you'll want to understand the pricing in relation to what you might be selling. Don't simply estimate but calculate every possible selling cost, at least as best you can at this early stage.

- If you're investing, you may want to write up a business plan to evaluate feasibility and profit potential.

- If you're a first-time buyer, it's recommended to first qualify your income. Determine the size of your down payment, then work out a monthly debt load so you can determine a comfortable price range.

3. IDENTIFY YOUR IDEAL DEVELOPER.

Like all tradesmen, developers and builders vary in their fields of expertise. For example:

- Some builders specialize in low-rise buildings.
- Some builders are known for their innovative use of space in high-rise projects.
- Some are well-known for offering exceptional deals during the sales period.

It's ideal to determine your own specific needs or preferences and focus on those developers that best address your requirements.

4. GET THE FACTS ABOUT THE DEVELOPER.

Before even signing, check out the reputation and financial strength of the developer. Ask your agent or the developer for "spec sheets" on the condo features, covering everything from floor plans to maintenance fees to development levies, including parking availability and expected occupancy of your home.

5. CHECK OUT THE NEIGHBORHOOD.

Once you're comfortable with the developer and potential price, it's time to learn as much as you can about the community. Here's where you get outside and explore the neighborhood. Whether you're planning to live there, rent or sell for profit, you want to know:

· What amenities it has to offer.
· What else local land-use officials plan to build in the area, especially if there's vacant land nearby.
· The rules for the condo board or find out when they will be set up.
· How commuting routes and times will affect you or whoever will live there. You might not be concerned about it, but it can be a big factor if you want to sell or rent the unit.

6. PLAN AND CHOOSE YOUR OPTIONS AND UPGRADES.

The lower the base price of the condo, the more likely you have a lot more options and upgrades you can add. Options include items the builder installs during construction, such as a kitchen island, glass shower doors, and high-end finishes.

Upgrading means selecting quality above "builder standard" such as carpeting, ceramics, detailing, kitchen fixtures and appliances. Be sure to take advantage of builder incentives that offer free upgrades or credits off of the sale price. Remember, you can add fixtures and lights later and sometimes for less money.

7. NEGOTIATE.

Ask, always ask. Often, I find many investors don't realize that there may be room for negotiating price, upgrades or options. Typically, all units cost the builder the same, so be sure to inquire about special offer discounts or upgrade packages.

MAKE SURE YOU KNOW WHAT YOU WANT...

As simple as this may sound, I find many real estate investors get swamped not having a firm idea in their heads before they go out searching for a property. In fact, every buyer and investor have *two* properties competing for their attention:

the one that meets your needs, and the one that fulfills their desires.

Obviously, your goal is to find the *one* that does *both*. In the real world, however, this situation doesn't always occur.

Far too often people buy for the wrong reasons. They loved the view and the four giant bedrooms but overlooked the location of the nearest park or school for their kids. This adds time, travel and even frustration with the sudden need to juggle schedules or fight after-school traffic.

For example, Larry (name changed for privacy reasons...) was convinced he found the perfect preconstruction condo. It was on sale via Assignment. This is where you can purchase the contract from the original new condo buyer and step into their shoes to close with the builder directly. Larry was crazy about the building, and no matter what I suggested he wanted to live there. The building had an aristocratic name, but the location was so-so. We negotiated a ridiculously low price because the sellers were desperate and could not close. He was thrilled on closing day.

As it turned out, he bought the sizzle, not the steak.

Fast forward one year. Now Larry wanted to sell. The unit no longer met his expectations nor his need. The commute was long. He wanted more space.

Financially, it had been a huge win. In terms of lifestyle, it was a disappointment.

...

I could detail hundreds of similar examples of little details that were considered insignificant, only to be seen soon after as vitally important. That big eat-in kitchen may romance you with thoughts of large weekend family brunches, but the frustration of hours spent in travel during the week may leave you wanting nothing more than to put your feet up on the weekend, rather than host a crowd.

When buying a property, always identify and satisfy needs first. Never shop with stars in your eyes.

BUYER ADVANTAGES YOUR DEVELOPER MAY NOT REVEAL!

Developers want to make money. Of course, so do real estate insiders. That's why if you've found an area that's ideal for your investment, it's always worth talking with developer well after the initial preconstruction buying period to see if you can get preconstruction pricing in their building – and that goes for buildings even where construction is complete!

Here's a fact that developers don't like to talk about...some have newly completed condos available for immediate delivery. They may even be ready to move into within 30 days. If this is the case and the developer is highly motivated to sell, there's a good chance they're keeping that knowledge to themselves.

Why? Profit, pure and simple.

IMMEDIATE DELIVERY CONDOS ARE OFTEN AVAILABLE FOR MANY REASONS:

- The building is nearly complete and there will be "spec" units on the last floors.
- A contract on a condo has fallen through.
- Unsold penthouse units are only released for sale at the very end, close to completion.

Opportunities like these often come with financing incentives or free options like parking. Maybe they choose to offer these instead of lowering the price, as a way to appeal to buyers. Quite simply, there's a lot of opportunities out there.

Here's a wild but true story about opportunity for you...

Once, there was an incredible opportunity to buy an immediate delivery $3.4 million penthouse condo directly from the builder. It was on the 80th floor facing the Toronto Harbour for $2.4 million.

Yes, I tried to execute for myself. Unfortunately, I did not have the liquidity needed at that exact moment. I reached out to my client base. Most thought it was too good to be true.

Well, I lost and so did my clients. Some well-connected insider managed to buy it for $2.4 million, selling it 3 months later for $3.0 million. Using leverage, they only had to pay 20% down + closing costs which amount to $550,000. With preconstruction, if you're in the right place at the right time (and you answer my phone calls), you too could make $600,000 in only 3 months.

8. BE SURE THE CONTRACT WORKS IN YOUR FAVOR!

When spelling out the particulars of an agreement with your developer, ensure you protect yourself by having safeguards written into the agreement, such as:

· placing your deposit in trust with their lawyer.
· having an assignment option.
· allowing you the right to lease during occupancy.
· advance notice of the occupancy date and your cost of living subsidy for delays.
· an explanation of what the fine print means in the warranties of the developer.

9. FINANCING – FIND THE BEST OPTION FOR YOU.

Some developers, especially in high-volume communities that place a large number of loans, can offer special financing packages. However, because "home loan" lending is highly competitive, you have many financing choices other than those being offered by the builder. Shop around for everything, from rates to lender fees. Appraisals, inspections, surveys, attorneys and closing fees can vary as well, so you may find you want to shop around.

10. JUST BECAUSE IT'S NEW...DOESN'T MEAN IT'S PERFECT.

Yes, your new preconstruction condo will be new, built with modern, durable materials that require low maintenance and are stronger, quieter, and safer. But that doesn't make them perfect.

Always do a thorough PDI inspection. Then create a developer "punch list" from what you've learned to address any problems before closing. An experienced real estate agent can help you negotiate the best price and terms with the builder.

WHY REAL ESTATE INVESTORS DON'T GO IT ALONE

DID YOU KNOW?

Many real estate agents sell fewer than 5 homes a year! Low volumes like this make it difficult for them to afford the advertising and special programs you need to get the high profile you need to sell fast and for top dollar. There's also a chance that at this low level they can't afford to hire an assistant, meaning they're the ones running around trying to do all the components of the job themselves, which can create a frustrating sales process for you.

OR, HOW TO FIND THE BEST AGENT

Not all real estate agents are the same, especially in the world of preconstruction condos.

The right one gives you access to an incredible investment opportunity. The other has you missing those early opportunities, leaving you to buy at a higher, more public, price.

WHO YOU CHOOSE CAN BE THE DIFFERENCE BETWEEN SPENDING – OR SAVING – THOUSANDS OF DOLLARS

When your luxury vehicle needs repairs, you don't take it to just any garage. You take it to the one who knows the ins-and-outs of your style of vehicle. Likely, it's someone you trust.

Likewise, when choosing a real estate agent, you want to look someone to partner with – someone you can trust. Someone who knows that by placing your best interests at the center of his or her efforts, everyone wins.

This is why I always recommend the following questions for anyone in search of a real estate partner. These are very specific questions that will ensure you get the best representation for your unique situation, goals, and needs.

Frankly, some agents may prefer that you don't ask these questions. If you ask, they know they must answer. Their answers will give you a good idea about the outcome you can expect if you choose to work with them.

In the world of preconstruction condos, most real estate agents know they don't have the experience and connections. It's just a fact, right? In life, not all things are created equal. For you, the investor, hiring a real estate agent is like any hiring process, with you on the boss' side of the desk, working to make the best decision.

Finding the best partner – the one with the knowledge, connections and correct client-centric view – is critical, especially for what is a major financial decision. So, when you're looking, ask these questions.

WHAT MAKES YOU DIFFERENT?
HOW CAN YOU HELP ME BUY A PRECONSTRUCTION CONDO?

The real estate market is tougher than it was a decade ago. You need an agent who can help you find opportunities, be a real estate investment guide, and, if selling for profit, help you sell your property.

Take time to ask what things the agent offers that others don't. And get specific. If you want to buy preconstruction, ask about it.

WHAT ARE YOUR COMPANY'S TRACK RECORD AND REPUTATION IN THE MARKETPLACE?

Doesn't it always seem like everywhere you look real estate agents are boasting about being #1 for this or that or talking up the number of homes they've sold? If you're like most homeowners, you've become immune to much of this self-promotion.

After all, you might be asking yourself, *"Why should I care about how many homes one agent sold over another? The only thing I care about is whether they can perform for me."*

Selling is certainly important. However, if you're interested in preconstruction condos you need someone who both knows 1) how to sell and 2) has a great reputation and relationship with developers and builders.

HOW REAL ESTATE PROFESSIONALS MAKE PRE-CONSTRUCTION CONDOS INTO SOLID INVESTMENT PROPERTIES

IDENTIFYING THE RIGHT RENTAL TYPE FOR YOU, MAKING IT AN IDEAL PLACE TO STAY, AND SUCCESSFUL MARKETING STRATEGIES

THE WONDERFUL WORLD OF SHORT TERM RENTALS.

Once, in what now seems like a very long time ago, top real estate investors preferred long-term rentals.

How times have changed.

Short-term rentals are all the rage today. This is especially true in Canada, and specifically in a growing metropolitan area like Toronto, where demand for short-term accommodations continues to grow at an ever-accelerating rate.

Many real estate investors who enjoyed success with long-term rentals are switching to listing large segments of their property portfolios on short-term stays.

Why is this?

Demand. And value.

Companies like Airbnb have revolutionized travel and accommodations and in doing so have transformed real estate investment. If you're reading this, you already know the demand for short-term, non-hotel, accommodations are huge.

This is a big reason I love condos as investment properties. If you get them early, they're new, meaning up-to-date amenities and less work to get them ready to rent.

This goes for both long-term and short-term rentals.

So, should you look for long-term or short-term rental clients? The question you really need to answer is, which is right for you?

DO YOU LIKE THE BENEFITS OF LONG-TERM RENTALS?

Like long-term renters themselves, the benefits of this type of rental remains consistent. You get:

· Regular income
· Predictable rental values
· Trustworthy renters, plus you get to check out their credit/personal history before inking an agreement
· Limited marketing required
· They clean their own stuff (ie., bedsheets, more on that in a moment…)

LONG-TERM RENTAL DRAWBACKS TO CONSIDER…

Frankly, if you want a set-it-and-forget turnkey investment property that delivers consistent income with low involvement on your part, there are not a lot of drawbacks to long-term rentals.

However, there is one drawback that every Canadian investor should definitely consider. For anyone looking to make money, it can be big. Here it is…

You are currently limited to a maximum annual rent increase set by the consumer price index. At first, you might think that's no big deal until you consider…

Rental appreciation is 6-11% per year based on true inflation!

I guarantee, your maximum annual rent increase doesn't match inflation. Rent increases can be capped as low as 1.8 %.

Do the math. It doesn't take long for that long-term renter to become a source of long-term lost income opportunity. And I can't tell you how many investors have come to me asking how they might end their tenants' lease. (Hint: There really is no good way.)

Is this really a drawback? It depends.

If you like the stability a long-term renter offers, I say go for it. Long-term condo rental is still big business and a great way to make a regular income.

Just understand you're not going to make as much with annual rental increases capped below inflation.

Of course, now you understand why so many property owners in Canada have transitioned their holdings to short-term rentals.

ARE SHORT-TERM RENTALS ALL ABOUT MONEY?

Well, yes and no.

Short-term rentals are in high demand, which means better profit margins. In Toronto, the short-term rental business is a healthy and thriving investment practice.

And by thriving, I mean short-term rental returns are crushing long-term returns. "How much rent can I make, Montu?"

Double. So if you're market rent is $2,000 for a long-term rental, the rule of thumb is that you can make $4,000 on the short-term platform. In the right place, $10,000 gross per month.

That's not a typo. $10,000 is a very real possibility.

At first, you hear Airbnb and short-term rentals and you might think it's all about tourism. You might even be thinking, "Wait, I don't want to cater to tourists."

Not so fast…

Tourists are only one group of people keeping short-term rental properties across Canada full. Students, business travelers, professionals relocating for work, company executives and families in need of a short-term rental property represent only a few others who drive demand.

My guests have been business executives, doctors, lawyers, students, travelers, honeymooners (can you believe that?!), and families between homes.

The high demand means BIG returns. Like preconstruction condo investments, short-term rentals are hot!

Demand isn't the only factor driving these big returns though. The fact rates aren't fixed is key. Your rental fee is never capped.

Now, beyond returns, some investors have shared another benefit they've enjoyed with short-term rentals.

They like the social element. It's true. If you like to meet new people and be social with people you don't know – your guests – then the social aspect of short-term rentals is another benefit.

DON'T RUSH TO SHORT-TERM RENTALS YET...

The income potential for short-term rentals is unquestionably alluring. Before you decide this is the way to go, you should consider a few other factors and temper your enthusiasm with a healthy dose of reality.

First, unlike a long-term rental, it's regular work. Sure, you're going to make a lot of money, but you also have to clean up after your guests. I mean, you can hire someone to do the laundry and clean the place if you like, but you will have laundry and cleaning to do.

That's right, with a short-term rental, you take on the responsibility for cleaning the sheets. In my own experience, and it hasn't happened a lot, but I can tell you I've had a few times where I thought, "What on earth did you do to these sheets?!"

Let's just put it out there, yes, people will have sex in your place. Specifically, on those sheets that you're going to need to clean.

Now, my pro-tip on those sheets? If they're stained, replace them. You're making enough on the rental.

Beyond what people do in the place, there are other elements of work too. Cleaning and regular maintenance are part of it. Another part is hospitality. Yes, you or your property manager should greet your guests when they arrive, much like a concierge service.

The reality of short-term rental investment properties is that you need to approach it with a business mindset. It's the approach you'd need if you were renting out your home. It's the approach you'll need it if you're renting out a condo you purchased as an investment property.

If any of these elements don't appeal to you, the short-term rental market may not be your cup of tea. If anything mentioned here is no biggie, well, then, you're ready to take your first step into a high-demand, high-income potential market. All you need to do now is put all the details in place once your preconstruction condo is ready for visitors.

TIPS TO CAPITALIZE ON THE SHORT-TERM STAY TREND AND COLLECT TOP DOLLAR RENTS

I started renting my condos for short-term stays in 2013. It didn't take long and each one started bringing in $2,000-$2,500 **cash-flow** per month.

Ok, forgive me but I simply can't stress enough just how perfect condos are as an investment for the short-term rental industry! They are simply the easiest way to maximize your investment.

In the Greater Toronto Area (GTA), these condos are going up in desirable areas to live, work and visit. Being in the GTA, they rent for top dollar.

The key to it all is that you need to do it right. This means details from legal considerations to whether to choose a beige or yellow shower curtain.

Let's look more closely at what you can do to make your unit rent for top dollar.

KNOW ANY AND ALL LEGAL REQUIREMENTS

Different cities in Canada have different rules and requirements for anyone who wants to rent a home or condominium for short-term stays.

For example, as of this writing the City of Toronto is planning on implementing the following STR requirements: you need to register with the city and pay an annual $50 fee. Also, STR operators will need to collect the hotel tax (MAT) of 4% and remit to the city. Keep in mind long term tenants are permitted to rent out their units with their landlord's permission on Airbnb.

Another major requirement is that Toronto requires your Airbnb to be your primary home and does not let you rent the entire residence for more than 180 days per calendar year.

Fortunately, you don't need to be an expert. The real estate agent who assisted with the purchase of your condo should be able to provide some guidance to help you confirm current requirements you need to consider.

CHOOSE YOUR RENTAL AUDIENCE

Who is your ideal renter?

My ideal renters, for example, are couples 25 and older. You can use general demographics like age and marital or family status, but you can also cater to specific audience verticals like –

· Tourists

· Students

· Medical professionals (residents, interns, those in medical school)

· Contract workers

· Business people

· Families in need of short-term rentals

· Last-minute travelers

Where you buy might play a big role in who your rental audience is. A unit purchased in the business district may be ideal for corporate rentals while one near the convention center of the city is better directed to tourism.

If you have a specific audience you want to cater to, then that should play a role in deciding where to buy. It will also be important when considering the amenities that you will provide, and even how you decorate the place.

YOUR CONDO MUST BE A DESIRABLE PLACE TO STAY

With a short-term rental, it's not enough that your place is new. That may be fine for long-term rentals. After all, the renter will bring in their own furniture and décor.

Your short-term rental needs furniture, décor, and amenities. It must be appealing to the most discerning eye and emanate comfort. Most importantly, it must look in person just like it does in your promotional pictures your audience sees.

Nothing earns a bad review as quickly as a sloppy bathroom or even just the unit that looks nothing like the pictures that sold it!

Plus, people want to feel they are getting the best value for their purchase. As a renter of a short-term stay property, your goal is not to be like a hotel room. Your goal is to be their luxury home away from home. It's why people are looking at your rental instead of a hotel – they want the comforts of home when they're not at theirs!

Also, they are looking for an experience in a unique property, something cool and unusual. Have a fancy rug, or bold paintings …the way a wealthy person might live like.

In short, when renting a condominium – even if it's your part-time residence, the space must be cleaner, more comfortable, and neater than their own home.

Here are several tips, sorted by room, you can follow to create a desirable living space.

LIVING ROOM

I always seek to make the living room as comfortable as possible. It's where your guests will crash at the end of a long day, watch some TV or do some work. Here's what I recommend:

1. <u>Get a high-quality sofa</u>. It should be durable and comfy too. Whatever you do though, don't buy used furniture. I could tell you horror stories of people who went cheap and bought used. (Can you say bedbugs?)

2. <u>Paint colors</u>. Room color does matter. It creates a sense of home, so plain white, undecorated walls won't do. Now, you can't miss with blue; it's the world's most popular color. Some warm colors can work, but I'd be careful here. Yellow is warm but generally a color to avoid. And always avoid brown or hue in the brown spectrum – it doesn't appeal to the majority of people!

For a simple decorating plan that's sure to work, you can go with white walls highlighted by tasteful art and prints that add color to the room. This approach makes re-painting easy and affordable when needed and replacing a picture isn't hard either.

Accent walls can make a statement when done well. When choosing paint, go with a bright matte finish to make removing any stains easier.

3. <u>Accessories</u>. You'll also want to have a coffee table, side tables, lighting, chairs and, of course, a TV.

When you design, make sure your style matches your audience. If it's a diverse audience, you may want more classic than avant-garde.

BEDROOM

Some condos have more than one bedroom, so depending on the layout, you may need to designate a master bedroom. Of the two or three bedrooms, this one must be the most comfortable as it's the bedroom used in every stay. (Second and third bedrooms always get less use.)

Here's what I recommend for the greatest comfort:
1. Bed. The style of bed isn't important unless style is one of your selling points. The quality of the mattress, however, is key. A customer review that goes on about "how comfortable the bed was" carries a lot of weight with potential renters.

So, invest in a high-quality mattress. The same goes for pillows. And avoid feather pillows, some of your guests might be allergic to feathers. Bed sheets are always white. You will want to bleach them as part of the cleaning process.

2. Paint colors. Like in the living room, popular blues, white with plenty of art highlights, or pleasant pastels work well.

3. Accessories. Think about it as if you are decorating your own bedroom. What would you want? Add nightstands, desks, dressers, armoires, drawers, desk and desk lamps, and in today's world, make sure to include a charging port for phone, computer, and other electronics.

DINING ROOM

The dining room table should always be able to seat at least the maximum number of guests your listing says the rental can accommodate. Here you have more flexibility regarding the type or style of furniture.

A few other items to consider:

1. Floor. I personally recommend tile or hardwood for the floors. These surfaces are easier for you and your guests to clean. Carpet will eventually become a disaster after months or years of traffic.

2. Lighting. It should be inviting with an ability to provide abundant light or dim for a romantic evening for two, so feature a dimmer. I mean, you don't know that some happy couple won't choose your rental as the place for a romantic dinner followed by the dropping to a knee and a marriage proposal. In short, lighting should be flexible.

3. Accessories. Faux plants add depth to a room. Art and prints should be appropriate for a dining setting.

KITCHEN

Ok, so tile for the floor is a no-brainer here. For appliances, make sure they'll accommodate the needs of the maximum potential number of people who can stay there. Smaller rental units can have a smaller refrigerator and appliances. Larger units will need a big fridge and more appliances.

What else do you need in the kitchen? Here's what I recommend:

1. Cooking & Dining Utensils. Part of renting a home is to be, well, at home. For many, this includes cooking (like that lovely couple did who just got engaged while staying at your place). Provision with an appropriate number of plates, drinkware, silverware, cooking and cutting utensils, serving bowls and more. Really, anything you might have in your kitchen.

2. Cleaning Supplies. Guests who cook must also be able to clean. Provide ample cleaning supplies like dish soap, paper towels, and napkins, for example. Having a mop, sponge and other cleaning supplies in a closet is a good idea as guests staying longer may want to be able to clean the place up a bit too, especially if it's an extended "short-term" stay.

You don't need to be extravagant in the kitchen, but you will want to make sure you have everything your renter might need.

Ultimately, people want to feel at home. Given the ability to clean up after themselves, especially families, helps to create that feeling of home and a sense of ownership – even if it's temporary – that enhances their comfort and enjoyment.

BATHROOM

Of all the rooms, the bathroom demands the strictest eye. It must be stellar. On every visit, everything must look new.

A deep, thorough cleaning between visits is essential. Other elements I recommend include:

1. Room décor. Vanity, mirrors, and furniture don't need to be high-end unless that's the feel you're going for. They must, however, always look clean and new.

2. Consumables. You do need to provide soap, shampoo, and lotion. You may not be a hotel, but you should provide basic toiletries as a courtesy.

Also, make sure there's plenty of towels and replacement toilet paper and facial tissue.

3. Budget for touch-ups. Caulk and grout touch-ups keep the bathroom clean and looking new. Paying a professional to do regular updates is a good idea.

OPTIONAL AMENITIES TO ENHANCE THE VALUE OF YOUR GUESTS' STAY

Here we ask, is there anything else you can provide that will add to the comfort, luxury and enjoyment of your guests stay?

For example:

- Do you want to include a wine cooler?
- Will you offer ensuite laundry service, if available in your condo?
- If you have a patio, will you provide a propane grill?

These added amenities are where your imagination and business plan come together to create an unparalleled guest experience.

Now, one benefit of renting a condo as an investment property is you automatically get the bonus amenities provided by your condo association. At a minimum, this includes lawn care and the cleaning of public spaces which can be a bonus to your offer, but doesn't cost you any extra time, money or effort!

PROMOTE YOUR PROPERTY ON THESE RENTAL PLATFORMS

Once you've got your investment condo ready for tenants and guests, you need to tell people about your rental. I recommend using these three platforms.

Airbnb
When I started, 75% of my business came through Airbnb. Right now, it's the standard and there's really no equal anywhere. If you're going to list your property anywhere, this is where you start.

One big benefit that has set it apart from the competition is the damage deposits it requires your guests provide. This feature protects you against damage that might occur during their stay. If damage does occur (and is immediately and properly reported), Airbnb will reimburse you.

VRBO / CanadaStays / HomeAway
This site provided me with a good number of tenants when I first got started. In the subsequent years, they haven't kept up with Airbnb's pace, and the number of tenants has reduced to a trickle through them. Yet, people still use it so you should too.

Booking.com / TripAdvisor
These sites get a lot of traffic. And by a lot, I mean on the scale of hundreds of millions of visits per month. The upside here is visibility. The downside is you're competing with nearly everyone from big-name hospitality brands to other local short-term rental investors like yourself. Even if it's not a big source of guests for you, I still recommend listing with them.

ADDITIONAL MARKETING STRATEGIES TO KEEP YOUR RENTAL FILLED AND CASH FLOWING

Booking platforms are one form of marketing that will bring a steady flow of guests. But you don't want steady. You want maximum occupancy.

To achieve this, I've found several highly targeted marketing strategies that have worked to keep my condos filled and profitable. Where Airbnb brought me three-quarters of my initial business, most of the rest came from Facebook and Google Ads I ran.

To get the most for your budget, you need to be highly specific in who and where you target your ads. You wouldn't target ads to the entire city of Toronto, for example. Instead, you would want to target specific postal codes *and/or* demographics.

For my properties, I get highly specific. As I mentioned earlier, I prefer to target married couples twenty-five and older. For this audience, Facebook ads have proven most effective in terms of finding the best tenants and their value. Google Ads cost nearly double those of Facebook, yet, I still recommend running them as they have proven effective in capturing the remaining audience I need to keep my properties filled.

Ultimately, where you advertise depends on who your desired target audience is. If you want business tenants, then you'd focus on business sites and periodicals. For tourists, you might consider looking at local travel guides (online or yes, even in print!).

When it comes to marketing, it pays to get creative.

PROPERTY MANAGER FOR SHORT TERM RENTALS

In the short-term rental community, property managers will do everything for you - for a fee. The range of fees for services varies from 15% to 30%, depending on how much they have to do. My team has an ace crew of property managers that handle our clients' short term rentals, and they offer a Group Discount package for clients of Dhillon Realty Systems.

In fact, they are so good that one night my guests arrived late around midnight, and the keys were not working...They were trapped outdoors. So my manager got out of bed, drove down and helped them into the home. Now that's white-glove service that I could not have done myself.

If you'd like to learn more or would like to find out how we might be able to help you, contact us via www.dhillonrealtysystems.ca, or give me a call at 1-833-845-5674.

MY OBLIGATORY MAINTENANCE RECOMMENDATIONS

A big advantage of condominiums is how much maintenance you don't need to do.

- You don't need to check your foundation.
- You don't need to maintain the yard.
- You don't need to worry about the plumbing, at least in the walls.
- You don't need to inspect brickwork.
- There are no roof concerns.

That's all handled by the condo board.

Even so, I feel obliged to share some regular maintenance you should do after every guest visit.

1. Check windows, doors, and gaps for weather-stripping and caulk. They should be fine, especially in a new unit, but still, you should always check. Problems here lead to drafts in cold weather, higher energy (AC) bills and insects in warm weather. All of these will ruin a guest stay and produce bad reviews.

2. Bathroom(s), walls, furniture, and really every detail should be inspected and maintained between tenant visits. You can do this, or you can hire a team to check the place if you'd rather not do it yourself.

A maid service can put the place right and get it ready for your next guests while a handyman can run through a checklist and make sure all walls are patched, furniture is in good shape and seals around doors and windows are in place too.

TOP TIPS TO SELL A PROPERTY FAST AND FOR THE VALUE YOU WANT

FEATURING...

**SELLING ON YOUR OWN OR WITH AN AGENT PARTNER
MY 9 STEP SYSTEM TO FAST SALES AND BIG PROFITS
WHAT TO DO IF YOUR PROPERTY DIDN'T SELL**

AND

THE ONE LEGAL ISSUE TO WATCH FOR WHEN SELLING A CONDO

SHOULD YOU HIRE AN AGENT OR SELL THE PLACE YOURSELF?

To get the best price for any real estate transaction, you really need to work with a real estate agent. When the time comes to sell – whether it's right away or down-the-road, you might be thinking you want to give it a try selling the place yourself.

I get it. I appreciate the attractiveness of the idea of not paying a commission to a real estate agent.

But I'll say it again if you want to get top dollar when you sell real estate, you really need to work with a real estate agent. However…

If you're set on selling yourself, I'm not going to discourage you.

I do, however, want you to be armed with all the facts and considerations.

Effectively, you need to ask yourself, what is your time worth? Here's what I mean…

WATCH OUT FOR LOW-BALL OFFERS!

Even if you sell on your own, most buyers do use a real estate agent. Why? It doesn't cost them anything for this service (*i.e. the seller – you – pays the agent's fee*).

There's also the danger of low-ball offers. Many buyers, investors, and speculators who seek out *For Sale by Owners* are often in search of a bargain. The low-ball offers from these types of buyers will often net you a much lower profit in the long run.

When selling on your own, you must consider:
1. **Are you prepared to handle all the possible** aspects of negotiations, evaluations, showings and all legal requirements?
2. **Consider what it will cost you** to effectively market your home?
3. **What price will a buyer offer you** as a *For Sale by Owner* minus the costs identified in point 2 above? Is this net price higher than the price an experienced agent could net for you minus his/her commission? And will the buyer expect you to discount the value since they know you're not paying real estate fees?

Ultimately, if you're in the GTA and just want a professional to do all of the above and make your life simple, contact my team via www.dhillonrealtysystems.ca, or give me a call at 1-833-845-5674.

That way you can just relax, we do this every day.

TOP TIPS TO SELL A PROPERTY FAST AND FOR THE VALUE YOU WANT

Ask anyone who has ever tried to sell their own home and they'll tell you that from the moment the "For Sale by Owner" sign goes up, the phone begins to ring. Unfortunately, most of those calls aren't from prospective buyers. Rather, they're from real estate agents looking to get your listing!

A lot of details go into selling any property. It's a process that demands time. If you want the experience and to learn, it can be very rewarding (I love it…which might explain why I do it for a living!).

If you're just trying to save the commission, you might find the investment of time and resources will end up costing you more than the commission itself, or worse…the unit may not sell fast enough and end up losing value by sitting on the market too long!

To sell your property "by owner," you must do the following:

- Price it right
- Make sure your home is prepared to sell
- Have all necessary legal documentation ready
- Market your home effectively
- Stay objective during showings
- Pre-qualify prospects
- Negotiate knowledgeably but firmly
- Know your buyer
- Never move before you sell
- Know the reason you're selling – and keep it to yourself!

In the next chapter, I outline my 9-step process for selling a property. I as an agent follow it. If you want to successfully sell "by owner," I recommend you follow it too. It does require a bit of work. Of course, if selling real estate didn't, we wouldn't need real estate agents, would we?

If you do decide to hire a real estate agent, you want to make sure you get the right one. Now, I personally recommend contacting my team via www.dhillonrealtysystems.ca or calling me at 1-833-845-5674.

However, whether you call me or someone else, you should do your due diligence and ask the following questions.

WHAT ARE YOUR MARKETING PLANS FOR MY HOME (WHEN SELLING)?

How much money will this agent spend in advertising your property? In what media (newspaper, magazine, TV, etc.) does this agent advertise? Can the agent reach your target buyer?

WHAT HAS YOUR COMPANY SOLD IN MY AREA?

Agents should bring you a complete listing of both their own and other comparable sales in your area.

WHO CONTROLS YOUR ADVERTISING? IS IT THE BROKER OR AGENT?

If your agent is not in control of their own advertising, you're not in control of your advertising. Then, when you're selling, your home is invariably competing for advertising space, not only with this agent's other listings but also with the listings of every other agent in the brokerage!

ON AVERAGE, WHEN YOUR LISTINGS SELL, HOW CLOSE IS THE SELLING PRICE TO THE ASKING PRICE?

This information is available from the Real Estate Board. Is this agent's performance higher or lower than the board average? Their performance on this measurement will help you predict how high a price you will get for the sale of your home.

ON AVERAGE, HOW LONG DOES IT TAKE FOR YOUR LISTINGS TO SELL?

This information is also available from the Real Estate Board. Does this agent tend to sell faster or slower than the board average? Their performance on this measurement will help you predict how long your home will be on the market before it sells.

HOW MANY BUYERS ARE YOU CURRENTLY WORKING WITH?

Obviously, the more buyers your agent is working with, the better your chances are of selling your home quickly. It will also impact price because an agent with many buyers can set up an auction-like atmosphere where many buyers bid on your home at the same time. Ask them to describe the system they have for attracting buyers.

DO YOU HAVE A REFERENCE LIST OF CLIENTS I COULD CONTACT?

Ask to see this list, and then proceed to spot check some of the names. *I'm not saying you should confirm they are real people but...*

WHAT HAPPENS IF I'M NOT HAPPY WITH THE JOB YOU ARE DOING TO GET MY HOME SOLD? CAN I CANCEL MY LISTING CONTRACT?

When investing, you want to stay in control of your money. Taking this approach toward buying, renting, and selling real estate is essential to maximizing your investment.

Be wary of agents that lock you into a lengthy listing contract which they can get out of (by ceasing to effectively market your home) but you can't. There are usually penalties and broker protection periods which safeguard the agent's interests, but not yours.

How confident is your agent in the service he or she will provide you? Will he or she allow you to cancel your contract without penalty if you're not satisfied with the service provided?

The answers you get to these questions will help you find the right real estate agent partner for buying preconstruction condos, and really any type of real estate you might choose to buy.

Buyers are far more discriminating, and a large percentage of the homes listed for sale don't sell the first time. It's more critical than ever to learn what you need to know to avoid costly seller mistakes and sell your home fast – and for the most amount of money.

In my experience, the home or condo that sells for top dollar also sells fast.

There's a strong correlation between profit and speed when it comes to selling real estate. Top dollar sales come from reaching the right audience right from the start. And when you're in front of the right audience, you're going to get plenty of offers which keeps the price high.

I've taken this knowledge and found that there are 9 steps to selling like this, whether you choose to sell by owner or work with an agent. Following them, and making sure your real estate agent follows them too, positions you to sell your property for the price that you desire.

STEP 1. BE CLEAR WHY YOU'RE SELLING. AND KEEP IT TO YOURSELF.

While you need to "understand your buyer," you also need to "understand yourself."

Your reasons for selling affect everything from your list price to how much time and money you will invest in the property getting it ready to sell.

Knowing your motivation will help you determine what is more important to you. Different goals will dictate different strategies.

Whatever your reasons, it is very important to keep them to yourself. It's like poker. If your buyer learns why you want to sell, you place yourself at a disadvantage at the negotiation table.

When asked why you're selling, simply say, **"My (our) housing needs have changed."**

That's it. Nothing ever more needs to be said.

Additionally, regardless of why you are selling, you should never try to sell by a specific date. This adds *unnecessary pressure* and is a serious *disadvantage* in later negotiations.

STEP 2. DO YOUR HOMEWORK BEFORE SETTING YOUR LISTING PRICE.

Once you set your listing price, you've told buyers the maximum they'll have to pay to buy your place. You won't get more. This is why I spend a little extra time with my clients identifying the right offer price. This is not a step to be taken lightly.

Keep in mind, the average buyer is looking at 15-20 homes at the same time they are considering yours. This means that they have a basis of comparison. If your property doesn't compare favorably with others in the price range you've set, you won't be taken seriously by prospective buyers or their agents!

Once, a dear friend of mine felt his property was worth $100,000 more than other comparable properties. (Does this sound familiar?) There was nothing exceptional about it, except he felt the rear pond and the privacy it offered was worth a premium.

Unfortunately, the builder of the neighborhood neglected the pond and did not install a water movement pump. That together with low rainfall left a once beautiful oasis looking like a swampy mosquito breeding ground; once blue water was now a murky brown.

The feedback we received from buyers and all of the offers reflected this since the price of the neighborhood did not appreciate since the previous year. The house sat on the market for months. Eventually, it sold for slightly more than the first offer we received.

You need to evaluate the market, see what properties like yours sell for, identify the competitiveness of the current market (demand vs. supply) and compare these with your goals and needs.

STEP 3. THEN DO MORE HOMEWORK AND SET YOUR LISTING PRICE.

In my opinion, I believe your agent should do this for you. Of course, if you are selling on your own, you don't have an agent to do so. If you have an agent who won't, may I offer that you might want to find a new agent?

Look back 6 to 12 months and see what properties like yours have sold for in similar neighborhoods. Compare that with your research on the pricing of current properties listed. The more data you have, the better you'll price your property.

A couple of additional notes to consider when determining your pricing…

- **Tax assessments are NOT a valid way of evaluating a home's value**. Assessments are *based on many criteria that may not be related to property values*, so they may not necessarily reflect your home's true value.

- **Make room for negotiation**. Before settling on your asking price, *leave yourself enough room with which to bargain*. For example, set your lowest and highest selling price. Then check your priorities to know if you'll price high to maximize your profit or price closer to market value if you want to sell quickly.

- **Be familiar with the terms of your potential sale**. Contract terms are often as important as price in today's market.

- **Carefully budget your selling costs**. I recommend preparing a net proceeds sheet to calculate your best estimate of what you will take away from your home sale. Prospective buyers may request this kind of analysis of buying costs.

Once you've done this extra homework, you're ready to set the price.

This is critical. Set your price too high and it won't sell. Set it too low and you lose money or potential buyers may think there's something wrong with it.

At this point, it's always important to remember home prices are determined by marketplace fluctuations, not what you believe your property is worth.

Honestly, working with a real estate agent at this point can be very helpful as he or she will give you an honest opinion of what you want to list at. If you're selling on your own, getting an outside, objective opinion is recommended.

STEP 4. MARKET YOUR HOME EFFECTIVELY

Putting your property in front of the best audience is essential to getting top dollar for it. Of course, it will appear on a listing service. You don't want to stop there though. Merely listing it relies on buyers to find you. For the best results, you need to go out and find them.

Start by identifying where you can find your best prospective buyers. Knowing who you want to target and where to find them gets them in front of the eyes who want what you're selling.

A little market research goes a long way to big profits. You, or you and your real estate agent, should strategize on this before listing. Remember, with a condo, you can't simply put a sign on your lawn.

You might reach nearby buyers through a local newspaper. In the digital world, you need to take

advantage of listing services and other real estate platforms, like Zillow. You might even consider running Facebook and/or Google Ads.

For condos, out-of-town buyers should also be targeted. You'll need to research where those buyers can be reached and create a strategy to reach them.

Finally, you ABSOLUTELY need to ensure that someone is always available to answer the phone, pick up messages promptly, return calls, and be ready to give qualified prospects a tour of your home as soon as possible.

STEP 5. MAXIMIZE YOUR HOME'S SALES POTENTIAL.

As the saying goes, 'you only get one chance to make a good first impression.'

Corporate North America knows this. Each year companies spend billions on product and packaging design. Appearance resonates with a customer base. This goes for selling your property too.

How your property looks is critical. The look and feel of it creates a greater emotional response than any other factor. Fortunately, you can do a lot to ensure its best appearance.

First, never gloss over needed repairs; your prospective buyers won't. Your job is to ensure that your condo stands out and above the competition.

Before a showing, clean like you've never cleaned before. (Preconstruction condo buyers looking to sell the new unit for profit have it good here as the place is brand new, clean and requires little work!) Pick up, straighten, unclutter, scrub, scour and dust. Fix everything, no matter how insignificant it may appear.

And make sure there are no odors. Odd smells like traces of food, pets and smoking odors can kill deals quickly. If prospective buyers know you have a dog, or that you smoke, they'll start being aware of odors and seeing stains that may not even exist. *Don't leave any clues.*

Your ultimate goal? For your property to get a "WOW" response from every prospective buyer, whether they plan to buy or not.

And one more point on this…you should never follow a potential buyer around. Your chatter makes it hard for them to imagine themselves as the new owner.

The best way to do this is to stay physically in the background during a showing. If a prospective buyer says something negative about your home, it is better to counterbalance this point of view by illustrating the positives rather than becoming defensive.

Here's a truth you need to remember – 'Emotion is the enemy of profit.' Stay objective.

STEP 6. MAKE IT EASY FOR PROSPECTS TO GET INFORMATION ON YOUR HOME.

In all my years of selling, I've discovered that many of the marketing tools that the average real estate agent uses to sell homes simply don't work all that well. Traditional open houses are one example.

I believe this is because prospective buyers value their time as much as you do yours. The traditional open house makes getting information difficult or exposes a buyer to sales talk, where all they really want is to get information.

If we extrapolate this knowledge, we can see that like you, your buyer doesn't want to play phone tag, never get an email response or get a sales pitch in response to every question.

To address these concerns, I always recommend that ads you or your agent places go to a 24-hour prerecorded hotline with a specific ID# for your home. This gives buyers access to detailed information about your property day or night, 7 days a week, and without having to talk to anyone.

This approach has proven to lead to 3x as many buyers calling for information on your home!

STEP 7. KNOW YOUR BUYER.
During negotiations, you need to control the pace, buyer's interest and set the duration for the negotiation period. Negotiations should allow for adequate time to think and make good decisions, but you can't let an uncertain buyer hem-and-haw over the purchase.

If you're working with a real estate agent, this is his or her job. Either way, knowing your buyer keeps you in control of negotiations and informs your decision-making concerning how far you can push to get what you want – and help your buyer get what he or she wants!

Start by understanding your buyer's motivation.

- Does he or she need to move quickly?

- Is there a specific element of your property they are looking for?

- Does the buyer have enough money to pay your asking price?

These represent only a few of the questions you should explore to understand your buyer. The more you know, the better off you will be. For example, if you know your buyer:

This translates to more buyers calling and competing for your home which translates to a higher selling price for you.

Pre-qualification of prospects should also be part of this step.

You don't want to waste your time entertaining buyers who could never afford your home. As potential buyers express interest, research their financial steadiness including job security, salary, debts, liabilities and credit standing.

- You won't be offended by a low offer.

- You'll have a good idea whether that low offer is only a starting point for negotiations and that you should counter-offer, or if it's the most they can afford and you just need to say no.

- You're less likely to start negotiating with a buyer who's not qualified for financing to meet your asking price. It still happens, but it's less likely to.

STEP 8. MAKE SURE THE CONTRACT IS COMPLETE.

As a seller, you must disclose everything. Be a smart seller and go above and beyond the legal requirements to disclose all known defects to their buyers in writing.

Why go through all this extra work? If the buyer knows about a problem, he or she can't come back with a lawsuit later on.

So…make sure all the terms, costs, and responsibilities are spelled out in the contract of sale. It should include such items as:

- The date the contract was drawn-up
- Names of parties involved
- Address of property being sold
- Purchase price
- Where deposit monies will be held

- A date for loan approval
- Date and place of closing
- Type of deed, including any contingencies that remain to be settled and what personal property is included (or not) in the sale

Here is a partial checklist of forms that you may need as part of your contract:

- Seller Disclosure
- Mortgage Payoff
- Deposit Receipt
- Buyer's Cost Sheet
- Personal Property
- Property Survey

- Purchase Contract
- Loan Application
- Property Profile Fact Sheet
- Closing & Settlement
- Exclusion List
- Sellers Statement/Plot Plan of Representation

Finally, never diverge from the contract. One example might be if the buyer requests a move-in before closing. If it's not in the contract (and this specifically never should be!), don't do it. Just say no.

The savvy real estate pro never does anything that risks the deal falling through.

STEP 9. DON'T MOVE OUT BEFORE YOU SELL.

A lived-in home (that's neat and clean!) is easier for a potential buyer to imagine themselves living in. If you've been renting your condo, leave it furnished as you sell.

Studies have shown selling a vacant home is more difficult than one that is lived in. Buyers say empty homes look forlorn, forgotten, and less appealing.

If, however, it's new construction and an unfurnished unit that you've always planned to sell (for profit), then what should you tell them (so they don't haggle on price)?

Simple.

Just tell your buyer, "My needs have changed."

This statement is the only one you ever need when selling to answer any question regarding your motivation.

If you're still unsure and want a quick consultation to find out how a professional could make things easier for you, just contact us via www.dhillonrealtysystems.ca, or give me a call at 1-833-845-5674

7 DEADLY MISTAKES MANY HOMEOWNERS (AND THEIR AGENTS) MAKE WHEN SELLING

These mistakes aren't specific to condos or preconstruction condos, but for anyone selling, this is top competitive intelligence. Be aware of these, you're not likely to make the same mistake. You also have a competitive advantage, knowing how to best appeal to prospective buyers!

1. Failing to know why they are selling.

2. Not preparing the property for the buyer's eye.

3. Poor analysis leading to incorrect pricing.

4. Selling too hard during showings.

5. Signing a long-term listing agreement without a written performance guarantee.

6. Making it difficult for buyers to get information on their homes.

7. Failing to obtain a pre-approved mortgage for themselves (as needed).

I'm including this section in case you're getting this book in response to an all too common real estate problem. Your house didn't sell. Or, it isn't selling as you expected.

If you find yourself in this situation, don't be discouraged!

COMMON PITFALLS WHEN SELLING & HOW TO AVOID THEM

(OR, WHY SOME HOMES DON'T SELL)

There's a good chance the reason it didn't sell may have nothing to do with your home or the market.

I've found that often the reality is very different than our fears in situations like this. In fact, many times, I've found the properties that aren't selling are often one of the more desirable on the market!

Of course, this raises the question: What should you do to get your property sold?

First, you need to review your situation before you put your property back on the market. Ask yourself:

- How was my relationship with my realtor? Did he or she meet my needs, or were there communication problems?

- Was I a priority to the agent and did we approach this with teamwork, a unified focus and solid strategy? If not, it may be time to find a new agent; ideally, one who understands the need for this to be a partnership. (If you didn't have an agent, maybe it's time to find a good one?)

- How was my price? Was it too high or too low and working against me?

- Was the property always ready for showing and did it strike prospective buyers with a powerful "WOW!" factor?

- Did you have a solid marketing plan?

Next, get an outside opinion.

I'm not saying you should second guess yourself. Rather, another pair of eyes, looking objectively at your situation, may see something you missed. It happens.

So, don't be shy about seeking the honest opinions of others. You need to *be objective about your home's good points as well as bad*. Fortunately, your Realtor® will be unabashed about discussing what can be done to make your home more marketable.

Then, after you identify where gaps in your effort may have existed, recommit yourself to do what it takes to market your property to the right audience, follow the necessary steps and reset the price, if appropriate.

It's worth noting...professional real estate agents keep a list of other agents and buyers with whom they regularly keep in contact. Sometimes it pays to connect with a professional and benefit from his or her years of database building to bring a swarm of buyers through your property. More buyers equal more offers.

Finally, address those areas following the 9-step plan in the previous chapter to make sure you have all the pieces in place.

*Remember... **BUYERS ARE OUT THERE ...AND THEY WILL COME!***

THE STATUS CERTIFICATE

When transacting with resale condos, you will encounter a little thing called the Status Certificate. When you are buying a condo, you are buying a tiny proportionate share of ownership of the entire building's responsibility.

There is a crucial document prepared by the building manager that discloses the state of the building you are planning to buy. Here are the key features to look for in the Status Certificate:

Maintenance fees for your unit. Make sure they match what's on the offer.

Are the maintenance fees paid by the seller, or are they back owing?

Is the parking spot and locker a match to what you think you're getting?

Are there any judgments or collections against the condo corporation?

Are there any lawsuits against the corporation?

Are there any upcoming special assessments each unit owner has to pay? Sometimes a windows overhaul of a building can cost each unit owner $10,000 apiece... and your insurance won't cover that (believe me, I tried, they wouldn't do it.)

Here's a cautionary tale of what can happen - and the real importance of a Status Certificate.

Two months after I bought a condo unit, I received a letter from management. (It was sent to all the residents.) The letter stated that the heating and cooling system of the building had failed. The contractor who installed it was not going to honor their warranty.

Now, yes, the installer was sued and it went to court. In the meantime, however, the residents' welfare was in serious danger, especially with the extreme weather Ontario gets throughout the year.

So...another contractor was hired to quickly address the heating/cooling mechanism - at a cost of $1,380,000! This resulted in a special assessment being levied on all unit owners. My proportionate share of it was just under $10,000. We were given 28 days to deliver the money!

I immediately reached out to my insurer, TD Insurance company. They refused to cover it EVEN though I had purchased the Special Assessment Protection package, which was supposed to cover such special assessments handed down to owners. I remember angrily asking, "Why am I paying the extra premium if you won't cover me when I need you?"

The response, as it always is with insurers, was, "Mr. Dhillon, that particular endorsement does not cover wear and tear, and failure of the heating/cooling system is wear and tear."

"Isn't every special assessment from the cause of wear and tear?" I growled back in frustration. "Why else would condo owners need to pony up extra cash, just for the fun of it? Do you think we wait around for opportunities to make necessary repairs???"

Hard as I tried, I did not get covered by TD Insurance company. Needless to say, they happily collected my premiums.

My situation was unavoidable, but the point of this is, review the Status Certificate for special assessments. If you're not comfortable doing it yourself, have your lawyer review and disclose to you any surprises you might have missed.

THE ONE LEGAL ISSUE TO WATCH FOR WHEN SELLING YOUR NEW HOUSE

"When such a major investment is transferred from one party to another, even the subtle legal details need to be taken care of. If not, they can turn into major problems when not handled correctly."

Your contract will have a lot of legal items to address but there is one item you must specifically look out for when selling your house, even if it's brand new.

Hard to believe, right?

Well, when it comes to legalities, as the saying goes, you need to make sure all the "i's" are dotted and "t's" crossed.

The good news about this is that when you know what to watch for, you can prevent a small detail from becoming a major problem or a deal-breaker.

Your real estate agent can help. You should also have a good real estate attorney on your team. Together, they can help protect your interests, especially when it comes to **The Home Inspection Clause**.

WHY YOU NEED TO WATCH OUT FOR **THE HOME INSPECTION** CLAUSE

If you've been renting your house to a tenant, you can easily understand a buyer wanting a home inspection. "Certainly," you might be tempted to think, "no one's going to want that on a brand-new home though, right?"

Au contraire.

New construction may be new, but that doesn't mean it is perfect. And your buyer has a right to ask for a home inspection.

The Home Inspection Clause effectively says that the buyer has the right to rescind their offer if they were dissatisfied with the outcome of a home inspection.

This clause has killed more real estate transactions than the average agent would ever want to admit. In some cases, it's been used unfairly against the seller when a minor repair issue would give a buyer a legal loophole to their change of heart.

And yes, even minor repair issues can exist in new condos. Being new, they're easy to fix, but with this clause in place, you may never have the chance!

The added danger of this clause is that this technicality causes you, the seller, to lose both time and money.

- You might have declined other offers in favor of the one that is falling through (*offers which may now be lost forever*).

- You might also have missed out on great offers made during current negotiations.

- You're at risk of incurring additional costs now having the property on the market longer.

Now, I'm not saying it's not a good or necessary clause. Of course, it is.

You and your real estate agent just need to make sure that it reads in a way that gives the seller the option to fix any items that the home inspection flags. This wording protects both the buyer and the seller.

- The buyer is assured that the home they are buying meets objective structural standards.

- The seller is protected against the whim of a buyer who changes his/her mind.

I wouldn't mention this if all contracts were written fairly. Sadly, they're not.

Protect yourself.

Make sure you are working with a knowledgeable real estate agent and an attorney experienced in real estate matters to ensure your interests are protected.

It also makes sense to proactively take steps to guarantee you'll pass any requested home inspection.

HOW TO PASS ANY HOME INSPECTION WITH FLYING COLORS

If you're going to pass a home inspection easily, you must be aware of what home inspectors look for. What should you look for?

Home inspectors look at everything. There are, however, 11 specific trouble areas in a building, both in your unit and in the larger building itself, that can create problems for you. When selling, seek these out and make sure they're in good condition.

1. DEFECTIVE PLUMBING

Defective plumbing can manifest itself in two different ways: leaking and clogging. A visual inspection can detect leaking, and an inspector will gauge water pressure by turning on all faucets in the highest bathroom and then flushing the toilet.

If you hear the sound of running water, it indicates that the pipes are undersized. If the water appears dirty when first turned on at the faucet, this is a good indication that the pipes are rusting, which can result in severe water quality problems.

2. DAMP OR WET BASEMENT

An inspector will check your walls for a powdery white mineral deposit a few inches off the floor. A new building shouldn't have deposits, but you should look for any staining. This indicates a water problem. A mildew odor is almost impossible to eliminate, and an inspector will certainly be conscious of it.

3. INADEQUATE WIRING & ELECTRICAL

Electrical in your unit should have a minimum of 100 amps service, which should be clearly marked. Wire should be copper or aluminum. New construction must be up to code, so unless you've made any changes in your unit, you're probably going to be in good shape here.

4. POOR HEATING & COOLING SYSTEMS

Here is another area where with a new condo you should be just fine. If you're selling a unit you've done work on, you should check – or have checked – the heating and cooling system

5. ROTTING WOOD

This can occur in many places (door or window frames, trim, siding, decks, and fences). The building inspector will sometimes probe the wood to see if this is present - especially when wood has been freshly painted. In your unit, you will want to check around windows and windowsills, areas where wood can get exposed and suffer the most damage.

6. MASONRY WORK

An in-unit fireplace will get a lot of attention if you have one. Rebricking inside can be costly. If your unit does have a fireplace, the inspector will probably want to speak with the association maintenance personnel to ask about the "chimney" to ensure it's not clogged and there's no danger of carbon monoxide gas build-up in the unit.

7. UNSAFE OR OVER-FUSED ELECTRICAL CIRCUIT

A fire hazard is created when more amperage is drawn on the circuit than was intended. 15-amp circuits are the most common in a typical home, with larger service for large appliances such as stoves and dryers. The best approach in your unit is always to have electrical done to code. This way, it's never a worry when it's time to sell.

8. ADEQUATE SECURITY FEATURES

More than a purchased security system, an inspector will look for the basic safety features that will protect your home, such as proper locks on windows and patio doors.

Deadbolts on the doors, smoke and even carbon monoxide detectors in every bedroom and throughout the unit per code. Before purchasing or installing any new items (presuming they weren't included during building), check with your local experts so you know exactly what you need.

SECRETS OF FINANCING ON YOUR TERMS

A 3-POINT PLAN TO GET YOUR IDEAL FINANCING

POTENTIAL COSTS YOU MAY ENCOUNTER

THE 3 POINT PLAN REAL ESTATE PROS USE TO OBTAIN IDEAL FINANCING

Financing a preconstruction condo is a little different than buying real estate insofar as your initial deposit can stretch across several years.

Standard financing has you making the first 15% within the first year. The final 5% deposit is later made closer to taking ownership of the unit. It's at this time that you'd need to have your financing arranged for the balance of your unit.

You might believe real estate investors are loaded with money and can buy at will. Those I know would love if that were true. But it's not.

What is true? Real estate pros have a 3-point plan to ensure they have their financing in place when they need it.

It looks like this.

POINT 1. UNDERSTAND YOUR GOALS.

Establish your reasons for wanting to buy.

- Are you looking to live there?
- Is this an investment property?
- How long do plan to own it?

Consider also what type of payment you're comfortable with – this will help you understand which condos are in your price range.

Also, do you expect your income to change? (Specifically, you want to anticipate if there are any chances it will happen in a negative way… there's no worries if it goes up, right?!)

POINT 2. GET PREAPPROVED FOR A MORTGAGE.

There are a lot of benefits to preapproval. You're insured against rising interest rates. With a preapproved mortgage, if rates go up, you still get the preapproved rate, but if rates go down, you receive the lower rate.

Equally as important, you have peace of mind when talking with the developer. It gives the ability to speak from a position of strength.

Preapproval is easy. Most mortgage brokers can obtain written preapproval for you at no cost and no obligation. More than just a verbal approval from your lending institution, a written preapproval is as good as money in the bank.

Yet, while it's easy, I still recommend working with a mortgage expert. You can qualify good ones with the following questions.

· Can you get me quick, easy and FREE mortgage preapproval?

· Can I get preferred access to special low down payments, monthly payments, and interest rates?

· Can I get special advance notice of listings that computer-match my home buying criteria?

Plus, if you work with a mortgage expert, you may be able to access special low financing options. Working with expert real estate agents can also help you get certain negotiating advantages with lending institutions and open access to better-than-average rates.

This can make purchasing much easier and more affordable as you have a smaller down payment and lower monthly payments – all ideal if you're planning to use your condo as an investment property!

POINT 3. EXAMINE ALL FINANCING DOCUMENTS IN EXTREME DETAIL.

Financial contracts may be boring to read, but they can have a dramatic impact on your future. There's a tendency for every person to get excited when they qualify for funding, but you need to resist that urge.

Once those documents are put in front of you, it's time to be all business. There are a lot of details to investigate. I would point you to a few to make sure they meet your satisfaction.

- Know your prepayment privileges. Pre-paying your mortgage can save you thousands in the long-term and speed the profit potential of an income property.

- Identify your payment frequency options. Dividing your mortgage payments into halves or even quarters paid across a month can cut years from the mortgage, saving you money, reducing your debt load so you can buy more properties, and create profit faster.

- Find out if your mortgage is both portable and/or assumable.

   o A portable mortgage, **where available**, is one that you can carry with you when you buy your next home and avoid paying any discharge penalties. This means that you will not have to go through the entire mortgage process again unless you are making a move up to a much more expensive home.

   o An assumable mortgage is one that the buyer for your home can take over when you move to your next home. This can be a very powerful tool at the negotiating table making it much easier and more desirable for a buyer to buy your home and again saves you any discharge penalties.

KNOW ALL UPCOMING AND POTENTIAL COSTS BEFORE SIGNING

"The last thing you need are unbudgeted financial obligations cropping up hours before you take possession of your new home."

When buying a property, unexpected costs can quickly chew up your profit or turn a purchase into a stressful obligation or financial nightmare. Real estate pros prevent this by figuring all the potential costs, extra fees, taxes, and/or other additional costs into their calculations of affordability.

Some of these costs are one-time fixed payments. Others represent an ongoing monthly or yearly commitment. It's just better to know about them ahead of time so you can budget properly.

The following list includes everything you need to budget properly. Not all of the costs below apply to every situation; however, it's best to know about them as they may come up the more you buy and sell real estate.

APPRAISAL FEE
Your lending institution may request an appraisal of the property which would be your responsibility to pay for. Appraisals can vary in price from approximately $175 - $300.

PROPERTY TAXES
Depending on your down-payment, your lending institution may decide to include your property taxes in your monthly mortgage payments. If your property taxes are not added to your monthly payments, your lending institution may require annual proof that your taxes have been paid.

SURVEY FEE
When the home you purchase is a resale (*vs a new home*), your lending institution may ask for an updated property survey. The cost of this survey can vary between $700-$1,000.

PROPERTY INSURANCE
Home insurance covers the replacement value of your home (*structure and contents*). Your lending institution will request proof that you are insured as it protects their investment on the loan.

SERVICE CHARGES
Any new utility services, such as telephone or cable, may require an installation fee.

LEGAL FEES
Even the simplest of home purchases should have a lawyer involved to review all paperwork. Shop around, as rates vary greatly depending on the complexity of the issues and the experience of the lawyer.

MORTGAGE LOAN INSURANCE FEE
Depending upon the equity in your home, some mortgages require mortgage loan insurance. This type of insurance will cost you between 0.5% - 3.5% of the total amount of the mortgage. Usually, payments are made monthly in addition to your mortgage and tax payment.

MORTGAGE BROKERS FEE
A mortgage broker is entitled to charge you a fee to source a lender and organize the financing. However, it pays to shop around because many mortgage brokers will provide their services free to you by having the lending institution absorb the cost.

MOVING COSTS

The cost for a professional mover can cost you in the range of:

- $50-$100/hour for a van and 3 movers, and
- 10-20% higher during peak demand seasons.

If you're furnishing a new unit as a rental, you might want to include furniture delivery costs here as well.

MAINTENANCE FEES

Condos charge monthly fees for common area maintenance such as groundskeeping and carpet cleaning in hallways. Costs will vary depending on the building.

WATER QUALITY AND QUALITY CERTIFICATION

If the home you purchased is serviced by a well, you should consider having your water checked by your local experts. In some areas a fee may be charged; in others, it may not. Either way, it's always good to certify the quality of your water.

LOCAL IMPROVEMENTS

If the town you live in has made local improvements (*such as the addition of sewers or sidewalks*), this could impact a property's taxes by thousands of dollars.

LAND TRANSFER TAX

This tax is applied whenever property changes hands.

SO, ARE YOU READY TO MAXIMIZE YOUR REAL ESTATE PROFITS WITH A PRECONSTRUCTION CONDO?

Real estate remains one of the best and most efficient ways to make money. Preconstruction condos are currently one of the fastest and easiest ways to earn big profits.

IN THIS BOOK, WE'VE COVERED:

- **How to buy preconstruction condos**

- **Why you need to buy early to get the biggest profit**

- **The many benefits of living and/or renting your preconstruction condo**

- **How to sell fast and for the best return**

- **The secrets real estate investors use to get the best financing**

- **What to watch out for so you don't get nickeled and dimed on extra "fees"**

We've covered a lot, but with an opportunity typically only know to insiders, there's a lot to cover.

For years, these condos have been the golden goose of real estate insiders. They are the definition of a hot investment – buy low and sell high. (Or, even better, rent them out as an income property!)

And now you know what the savvy insiders know. Preconstruction condos can change your life and fill your bank account!

If you've been looking for an unparalleled real estate investment with incredible profit potential, I encourage you to consider this opportunity.

Just remember:

- To get in early and make the greatest profit, you need to find a real estate agent who knows preconstruction condo buying and selling and has the connections you need.

- You can arrange your own financing or sell your own property, but a solid team of professionals, specifically experienced real estate professionals, mortgage lenders, and a knowledgeable real estate attorney, can make investing in real estate easy and simple.

- Always keep the reason you're selling to yourself!

Preconstruction condos are an amazing opportunity. If I can help in any way, please do not hesitate to reach out. For more information, to learn more, or to find out how to enhance your wealth by millions of dollars, go to www.dhillonrealtysystems.ca, or give me a call at 1-833-845-5674.

ABOUT THE AUTHOR

Montu Dhillon founded [Dhillon Realty Systems](#) after years of fostering Developer relationships. He was a seasoned securities professional and stock market investor who changed his investing strategy to real estate in 2006. He is experienced with single family homes, duplexes, multi-families, and still holds them in his portfolio. He shifted his focus to condos in 2015 when, using market principles he calculated the Toronto condo market was undervalued and ripe to rally. Consequently he bought several condos in prime areas and counselled clients to do the same. Since then he has traded hundreds of properties and offers white glove investment help for people looking to diversify their portfolios with the easiest asset class in real estate: Condominiums.

Offering market, rental, and location analysis, Montu has helped savvy investors achieve staggering returns by soliciting incredible deals via his Platinum Broker connections. He believes the condo rally has just started, and we will see the Manhattanization of Toronto in the next decade.

When he is not working, you can find him camping, golfing, and visiting buffalo farms. In a tightly contested vote, he was recently named Best-Dad in the World by his wife and two children.